The Poetry Connection

The Poetry Connection

An Anthology of Contemporary Poems with Ideas to Stimulate Children's Writing

By Kinereth Gensler and Nina Nyhart

Teachers & Writers Collaborative

5 Union Square West, New York, N.Y. 10003

The publication of this book is made possible by a grant from the Na-
tional Endowment for the Arts in Washington D. C., a federal agency.

Acknowledgements continue on page 213.

Library of Congress Cataloging in Publication Data
Main entry under title:

The Poetry connection.

    Includes indexes.
    1. Poetry and children. 2. Poetics—Study and teaching. 3. Poetry
—Collections. 4. School verse. I. Gensler, Kinereth   II. Nyhart, Nina.

PN1085.P58   811'.5'4   78-14926
ISBN 0-915924-08-0

For our children
Orin, Daniel and Gail Gensler
Nicholas, Lynn and Andrew Nyhart

CONTENTS

PREFACE

This book grew out of our experience as poets teaching workshops in Massachusetts schools. To help children write poems, we tried out many current teaching techniques and found that one of the most effective was to present selected poems by other children and by professional poets. From these poems the children could extract elements that engaged their individual interests and that they could make use of in their own writing.

Over a period of five years we developed a collection of such "model" poems. They were selected from books by contemporary poets, literary magazines, an assortment of modern anthologies, and from children's classroom writing.

Discussions with teachers revealed a widespread interest in such a collection and in a complementary text that would suggest ways to use the poems. We got on-the-spot reactions from teachers whose students we were working with. In addition, we were able to try out and discuss a wide range of poems in poetry writing workshops we conducted especially for teachers.

We are particularly indebted to Anne Martin for her example of the role that an inspired classroom teacher can play in forwarding creative writing in general and poetry in particular. We value her long-standing interest in and support for this book. To her, and to Diane Lowe, our thanks for sharing their students' poems with us.

For implementing teacher workshops we acknowledge with thanks the work of Edward Yeomans of The Greater Boston Teachers Center and Norman Colb, Director of English in the Brookline Public Schools.

Our appreciation also to the Massachusetts Council on the Arts and Humanities, which for a number of years helped to fund our teaching in its Poets-in-the-Schools program in the following Massachusetts schools: Devotion School, Brookline; Juniper Hill and Hemenway Schools, Framingham; Medway Elementary School, Medway; Congress Street and Spruce Street Schools, Milford; Broad Meadow School, Needham; Cottage School, Sharon; Woodward School, Southboro; West Junior High School, Watertown. Our thanks to the superintendents of schools in these communities and to the principals and teachers we worked with.

We were also fortunate in being able to teach under the auspices of Arts/Six at Brookline High School and in two private institutions: Beth El Temple Center, Belmont, and Roxbury Latin School, West Roxbury.

We especially thank the children we taught. Some of their poems appear in the anthology section of this book.

Finally, we owe much to our friend, poet Ruth Whitman, who was the first artistic director of the Massachusetts Poets-in-the-Schools program, and subsequently president of Poets Who Teach, Inc. Her generous encouragement has sustained us for many years. We are grateful to her and to our fellow poets in these groups who, by sharing ideas, created an exciting climate in which to work.

Kinereth Gensler
Nina Nyhart

INTRODUCTION

Poets know that reading poems by other authors often triggers their own writing, that poetry itself generates new poems. As poets teaching poetry writing workshops in schools, we have learned that children, too, can discover this connection, and that one excellent way to turn kids on to writing is to show them a variety of evocative poems.

In the process of collecting model poems for this purpose, we realized that the poems in anthologies for children are selected for pleasure and entertainment, rarely for the particular quality we were looking for—the capacity to start an original poem moving within a child.

This book is a special kind of teaching anthology. It contains ten chapters, each of which focuses on a way to spark the writing process in children, and a closely related anthology of poems by both adults and children.

The chapters vary in emphasis. Some stress form, others emphasize experience or imagination, many incorporate ways to deal with feelings. Poems from the anthology are frequently cited to illustrate ideas in the text; a few poems are discussed more fully. At the end of each chapter, a comprehensive list of pertinent poems in the anthology is provided. The last chapter, "More Connections," includes additional groups of poems that might serve as the bases for other teaching units.

The anthology, divided into two sections, consists of an expanded compilation of those poems that we have found trigger the writing process most successfully in children. In the first section, the poems are by adults (mostly modern American poets); the second section consists of poems by children (mostly our own students in grades 2 through 9).

How the Poems Were Selected

In choosing poems that would stimulate children to write their own, we focused on three criteria:

1) Is there something immediately appealing about the poem: its shape, title, a particular word or phrase?

2) Does it contain specific elements that can get children started on their own poems: a strong feeling that reverberates, a particular poetic technique, a way to play with words, subject matter that the child can explore?

3) Is the poem good enough to stand up under repeated readings? Does it remain evocative?

We applied these criteria to the poems of established, professional poets. They were also applied to the children's poems; however, we view the children's poems as stages in a developing process rather than as polished artifacts. Most of these poems were written quickly in class; few were revised.* The anthology includes a large selection of poems by children because the concerns and feelings of peers tend to be highly contagious. Reading poems by other children moves children to write their own.

How Model Poems Work

There is no one "correct" way for a child to make use of a model poem. Different elements of the poem will appeal to different children: one student will pick up an aspect of the form, another will be turned on by the subject, a third will be entranced by a particular line. Some children will write a close imitation of the whole. The sudden recognition of a poem's emotional wallop makes some children want to become poets, too. Sometimes the response is hidden. Ideas and possibilities are being stored up, to be incorporated into poems written at a later date.

A wide variety of spin-off poems can be anticipated, for example, from May Swenson's "Bleeding." A child might respond to this poem by writing a conversation, or a poem about a knife, or a poem employing the persona device (see Chapter VII), or a shaped poem. The title alone might be borrowed to begin the child's own poem.

Some children's responses to model poems are: "I want to write a poem like that"; or, "I could write a poem like that"; or, "I want to write my own"; or, "I can't do that." We have made every effort to exclude from this collection poems that are likely to elicit the "I can't" feeling. Poems that are technically or intellectually too sophisticated make children feel inadequate, stymied when it comes to their own writing. Many of the poems in anthologies for children, ones which children enjoy listening to, fall into this category.

Ways to Present Model Poems

Poems are meant to be seen as well as to be heard. Part of what makes a poem a poem is the way it looks: the length of its lines, how the words are spaced on the page, how it is punctuated, whether it has stanzas, its over-all shape. Some ways to help children examine the visual aspects of a poem are: 1) to give each child a copy of the poem; 2) to pro-

---

*Except for spelling corrections, the children's poems have remained unrevised. Where a misspelled word is an integral part of the poem, as in "Z is a zerox machine", we have left it unchanged.

10

ject a transparency of the poem by overhead projector; 3) to write the poem on the board (or on large construction paper). In addition, model poems can be put up around the room, and books of poetry made available for browsing.

It is essential for kids to hear a poem as well as to see it. Teacher and children can take turns reading the poems slowly out loud. Listening to poems on tapes or records can expand the sense of the way a poem sounds.

How many poems to present in any one workshop depends upon the context. Sometimes one poem will do the job. Poetry is rich fare; too many poems presented too closely together can be indigestible. Ways we have introduced model poems include:

1) Group discussion of a topic like dreams or animals, including the sharing of experiences and feelings, followed by presentation of related poems by both children and adults.

2) Examination of concrete objects brought into the classroom, followed by presentation of an evocative adult poem (e.g., Sylvia Plath's "Mushrooms" together with some real mushrooms).

3) Explanation of a particular poetry writing technique (e.g., acrostics or messages) by presenting a number of such poems.

The next step is for students to write their own poems. They are much more likely to respond creatively to the models when they sense that their teacher is truly interested in the poems selected. A good rule-of-thumb is: don't pick poems as models that you yourself don't like. If you like the poems enough, you might be moved to write a poem in class along with your students, and that would be an added bonus, for them and for you.

WAYS TO WRITE POEMS

CHAPTER 1

ACROSTICS

One way to begin the process of writing poems is to try out a specific poetic form. The acrostic, which has a "spine" of letters running down the left-hand margin, provides an interesting and accessible form for beginners. The initial letters of the lines, when read downward, spell out a word or a phrase, sometimes a name. For children in the early grades, the following acrostic provides a clear example:

> Jumping
> All over the
> Candlestick. Now you
> Know my name!

By choosing the vertical, key word, the child is able to control the subject and the length of the poem. With the framework of the poem already set up, a writer feels more secure and has a sense of direction. But because the controlling factor for each line is, after all, *only* a letter and not a word or a rhyme, the acrostic form allows for a great deal of freedom.

Many children are relieved to realize that rhyme at the end of the line is not a necessary component of poetry. Skillful and satisfying rhyme is hard to do, and it is good for kids to know from the outset that there are other ways to construct a poem.

The range of subject matter that can be written about in the acrostic form is extremely wide. Children often select as key words proper names that have special meaning for them and that provide built-in subject matter (see "Craig" and "Colorado"). Sometimes, choosing the name of an emotion makes that emotion temporarily more manageable (see "Fear" and "*Left out of all the little intimate conversations*"). Some children use the acrostic form to handle a serious or highly personal subject in a slightly disguised way (see "*K is for knob on a door to open,*" "Mud," and "A Pencil").

For easy reference, all poems cited in this chapter are listed, with page numbers, at the end of the chapter.

Acrostics can serve to start a child writing the way many poets do, by allowing the words to lead them, to be the keys to discovering what it is they have to say next. The eighth grade student who wrote "Someone is walking through the snow" trusts the word *snow* to lead her through the poem just as the walker in the poem trusts the "real" snow to lead him. The poem becomes a snow-directed journey in which form and content are meshed. The challenge of the key word may be all that it takes to elicit highly original writing. (Also see *"Water falls."*)

For some children, particularly those who enjoy puzzles, the acrostic form is simply fun, incorporating as it does the notion of a secret message hidden inside the poem.

Occasionally, a poem that begins as an acrostic winds up as a "regular" poem. Sometimes the child goes off on a tangent, abandoning the acrostic scheme for another poem that insists upon emerging. Rather than try to "fix up" weak or irrelevant lines in an acrostic poem, a child may decide to remove such lines in order to make a stronger poem (see "Bicycle").

The acrostic is an old poetic form used in the Book of Psalms, in medieval liturgy, and in nineteenth century valentines. Modern poets have revived it from time to time. Accessible to almost all age levels and quickly explained, it seems today to be a most useful and appealing form for a great many children.

See:

CHAPTER II

THE SOUND OF A POEM

Sound is a powerful tool for the poet. Reading aloud a poem such as Roethke's "Old Florist" demonstrates that how a poem sounds is an important part of its being. In poetry as in music, what pleases the ear has changed somewhat over the centuries, but the poet's need for words that "sound good" remains. Children, too, are fascinated by and enjoy playing with the sounds of words. They discover that sound is one of the elements of a poem that makes it hang together and makes it memorable.

To create a satisfying constellation of sounds, poets often use one or more of the following devices: 1) rhythmic beat, including the cadence of natural speech; 2) onomatopoeia and alliteration; 3) rhyme and off-rhyme; 4) repetition.

Rhythm

The rhythm or beat of a poem works particularly well when it is related to and reinforces what is being said in the poem. The regular metrical pattern of "Counting-Out Rhyme" makes it a good chant to bounce a ball to or choose teams by. "We Real Cool" and "Panther" gain dramatic power through their strong, syncopated beat. The quiet, mysterious and somewhat ominous quality of "Mushrooms" is reinforced by its sound-pattern and its insistent rhythm.

In poems that imitate the cadence of natural speech, the length of the lines is often determined by natural breath units (see "This Is Just To Say," "Knoxville, Tennessee," "Dog Talk," "The Baseball Dream").

Onomatopoeia and Alliteration

Sensitive and inventive second graders, aware of the sounds around them, come up with poems like *"Water falls"* and *"Rain sounds like machine guns."* Quite spontaneously, these children have incorporated onomatopoetic language (words that imitate the sound associated with a thing or action) into their poems.

For easy reference, all poems cited in this chapter are listed, with page numbers, at the end of the chapter.

Alliteration (repetition of initial consonant sounds) is used with obvious enjoyment by a second grader in *"Clap clop"* and by an eighth grade student in "Sipping Ice Cream." Adult poems rich in alliterative word play include "Cape Ann" and "Pomander."

Rhyme and Off-Rhyme

For children with a good ear, rhyme sometimes occurs naturally and adds to the total enjoyment of the poem (see *"Where will I go,"* "Panther," and "Mathematics"). However, when rhyme is a formal requirement it is apt to become a trap for all but the most skilled poets; instead of opening up the possibilities of poetry, it shuts them down. Children have limited vocabularies. Caught in the bind of not knowing enough appropriate rhyming words to choose from, they too often end up writing things they do not mean and that they themselves say are "stupid."

A wider range of sounds is provided by off-rhyme (also called slant rhyme, half-rhyme and near-rhyme)—that is, by words that sound partially alike and sound pleasing together. The pairs of long and short lines in Mark Strand's "Sleeping With One Eye Open" provide an excellent example of various kinds of off-rhymes. For children who love to rhyme, reading aloud the Strand poem, "Counting-Out Rhyme," and others among the poems listed below demonstrates the elasticity of off-rhyme.

Repetition

Repetition is a basic ingredient of poetry. For children, a pattern that makes use of recurrent words or phrases is both pleasurable and manageable. The pattern can consist of repeating a single word ("Sea-Wash") or a phrase ("Fair Catch," "We Build Toward The Sky") or an entire line ("The Magical Mouse," "Rattlesnake Ceremony Song"). Sometimes a stanza is repeated, usually with variations ("Ballad of Red Fox"); sometimes a question is repeated (as in "Where Did He Go?"). With each repetition, meaning becomes intensified.

Louise Bogan's "Train Tune" is built out of—and depends almost entirely upon—a repeated phrase. The words "back through" which begin most of the lines, simulate the rhythmic, hypnotic clickety-clack of train wheels. Children might base their own poems on impressions that come to them from the rhythm of familiar repeating sounds: footsteps, windshield wipers, waves, pulse beats, drums, jackhammers, etc.

As a total experience in the elements of sound play, "Shaman's Incantation To Exorcise A Demon" is a fascinating poem for children to

18

read aloud. It incorporates many of the elements of sound discussed in this chapter: various kinds of repetition, rhythm, and the imaginative, onomatopoetic use of animal sounds.

See:

CHAPTER III

THE SHAPE OF A POEM

Poems take their shape from the way words are arranged on the page. One familiar pattern is the grouping of lines into stanzas, as in "The Bird Of Night," "The Ballad Of Red Fox," "Mushrooms," and "Where Did He Go?" Another arrangement is to shape the poem so that its visual appearance is more closely related to what is being said.

Even a poem in stanzas may send strong visual signals. In "Train Tune," the repeated phrase "back through" creates a visual image (the suggestion of vertical train tracks and horizontal ties) that supports the meaning of the poem. In "Clock" the receding margin reinforces the idea of drifting and of time and twigs being swept away.

Some poems gain power and interest from an irregular placing of lines and words on the page and from the open spaces created by such an arrangement. Ferlinghetti's *"Fortune has its cookies to give out"* serves as a useful model. In addition to scattered lines that attract the eye, Ferlinghetti uses other visual devices in this poem: placing a single word on a line, capitalizing a key word ("FIREMEN"), and suggesting with words the path of falling water.

Children, too, spread their poems out on the page. In the fourth grader's poem, "Where Will I Go," the words cluster around the pivotal word *or*, and the poem winds up with the singular *me*. The appearance of this poem reflects its movement: from a contemplative question about death, to an engaged feeling of loneliness, ending in a plea ("come with/me").

Lou Lipsitz's "Skinny Poem," with its one-word lines, has instant appeal for some students. Shape and meaning go together to make a serious statement. Aspects of the poem that make it intriguing for children seem to be: 1) the eye-catching title; 2) the comforting thought that a poem can be "skinny," made up of simple, one-word lines; 3) the notion of personifying a poem, talking to it, giving it ribs and legs. (For other "persona" poems, see Chapter VI.)

For easy reference, all poems cited in this chapter are listed, with page numbers, at the end of the chapter.

The impulse to "show" and "tell" simultaneously can lead the poet to choose a pattern that focuses attention on the parts of words—syllables and letters. For example, the eighth grade student who wrote "Drip, Drip," a small poem about a drop of water, could have arranged his words in neat, haiku-like lines:

A drop of water
falling into a pond,
splash!

He did not choose to do so. Instead, he created far greater dramatic impact by breaking up the parts of the words and dribbling them down the page.

Other effective ways to play simultaneously with meaning and with the parts of words—making anagrams out of them, shaping, rhyming, linking and unlinking them—are suggested by "Pomander" and "Mathematics."

Some intriguing poems in which meaning and shape go hand-in-hand are May Swenson's "Bleeding," with its jagged slash, her "How Everything Happens," a poem based upon wave patterns, and Edwin Morgan's "The Computer's First Christmas Card," designed to look like a computer printout. Children's poems that effectively match shape to the sense of the poem are *"I am a sandune at,"* "Twinkle," and "What Am I?"

Some shaped poems are like paintings: they must be seen to be appreciated; their power comes from their immediate visual impact. Such poems are called *concrete poems*. Reinhard Dohl's apple poem has a hidden surprise that is fun to discover.

Two interesting concrete poems by students are "Snakes" and "Wave." The poem "Mirror," written in mirror-writing, exists in some borderline world of its own.

See:

CHAPTER IV

DRAWING ON EXPERIENCE: THE SENSES, MEMORY

Poets are closely attuned to their own senses, to the experience of the moment, and to vivid recollections from the past. Children need to know that sensory experience can be talked about—that it "belongs" in poems.

One way to increase children's awareness of their own sense perceptions is to bring into the classroom objects designed to trigger memory responses. To direct attention to the sense of smell, for example, cloves, vanilla, fresh earth, vinegar, etc., can be introduced, and the children encouraged to talk and write about how these affect them. This kind of experience can be presented together with a model poem such as "The Cellar." Or a variety of fruits and vegetables can be brought in, and the children encouraged to smell, touch, taste, and observe closely. The question "What does it remind you of?" often starts a child writing.

Using a blindfold accentuates awareness of the sense of touch. When children have to feel their way around a room or out-of-doors, their touch perception becomes more important. Also, objects with special tactile qualities can be brought into the classroom: sand, polished stones, ice cubes, a brick, a Ping-Pong ball, a silk scarf, a feather, etc.*

The sense of sight is sometimes taken for granted, yet many poets gain insight through careful attention to the visible world. Looking closely can reveal beauty in an unlikely situation ("Between Walls"), can produce a sudden insight ("Lying In A Hammock At William Duffy's Farm

For easy reference, all poems cited in this chapter are listed, with page numbers, at the end of the chapter.

---

*When you bring outside catalysts into the classroom, there is always the chance that the stimuli will eclipse the writing process. But, in the long run, recognition that sense perceptions belong in poems is valuable to the ongoing creative process.

In Pine Island, Minnesota"), can lead to questions, including the search for meaning ("Sky"). Careful observation can result in a simple simile (*"Rain sounds like machine guns"*), a detailed portrait ("Old Florist"), or a complex system of seeing and thinking ("Thirteen Ways Of Looking At A Blackbird").

Photographs and reproductions of paintings also stimulate the sense of sight. The child can write a poem "to go with" the picture, or the poem can be written from the inside out—in the voice of someone or some object in the picture. What are the smells and sounds inside the picture? Some poems written to accompany photographs are "Protector," "A Wonder," and "Where Did He Go?"

The stimulus of sound in the classroom often starts a poem moving. Poems can emerge from listening to whatever is going on at the moment (see "I Hear" and "The Class Of Poems") or listening to recordings of music or of natural sounds such as whales, wolves, the ocean, a wind harp, etc. A wide variety of poems, many of them incorporating fantasies, are written from such aural stimuli (see "Sounds Of The Whale" and "Copland's Jazz Concerto").

In addition to making use of immediate sensory experiences, a poet draws on a unique fund of memories. Children as well as adults can make use of this source to retrieve original material for poems. Calling on one's memories helps to define a sense of self and to build up a "vocabulary" of personal images and key words.

Some poems pin down memories by "naming names"—that is, by telling the name of a place or a person that contains a particular emotional charge for the poet. A place name often calls up special feelings through remembered sensations—smells, sights, tastes, and sounds (see *"Fortune has its cookies to give out,"* "Knoxville, Tennessee," "The Cellar," "Colorado"). The name of a person may help to anchor remembered experience, as in "I Hate My Crib" and "Sam's World."

Powerful, vivid memories are sometimes described in detail (see *"Fortune has its cookies to give out,"* "Listening To Grownups Quarreling," "The Portrait," "Supper," "Going, Going, Gone," and "Where Did He Go?"). A memory may also be recounted very briefly (see "Poem" and *"me beside the door"*).

By seeing model poems that deal with common childhood experiences (going to a favorite place, witnessing a family argument or dinner scene), children discover that their own past experiences are legitimate subjects for poems.

See:

CHAPTER V

FANTASIES AND DREAMS

Poets rely heavily on the part of the mind that asks "what if?"—that speculates and fantasizes. Many poems are written in a state of reverie, when the imagination is given free rein.

One of the most effective ways to help children tap this rich source within themselves is to show them poems in which all sorts of imaginings are expressed. These include daydreams and nightmares, exaggerations and outright inventions. The kind of figurative language that compares dissimilar things, creating similes and metaphors, also springs from the imaginative activity of the mind. Looking at model poems, kids discover that they are in a time-honored tradition when they take odd leaps in their writing.

Some poems describe the process of leaving the everyday world behind and moving into reverie (see "Clock" and "Drifting"). Others plunge directly into an imagined "what if?" situation (see "Simultaneously," "Stone," "The Key To It All," and "Unicorn"). One way to encourage such dreamings-up is to suggest the invention of something: e.g., a new kind of animal, as in "Birdaggators Birdaggators," "Self-Portrait As A Bear," and "First Lesson."

Some poems are based on exaggerating, on seeing what it would be like *if* something outrageous occurred (see *"I am the tallest woman in the world"* and "In The Lobby"). Telling such a "lie" stretches the imagination and allows an ambition, a dread, or a secret wish to be expressed in words. Sometimes, too, dreams can be fulfilled (see "The Baseball Dream" and "To Paint The Portrait Of A Bird"). Other poems explore certain kinds of intriguing transformations ("Mirror," "*It melts*," and "And With The Sorrows Of This Joyousness").

Just as life and death are basic concerns for adult poets, so ideas about being born and dying are part of children's fantasy life. Given encouragement, some children are glad to get these thoughts down on paper. Providing a list of open-ended first lines sometimes helps to get a

---

For easy reference, all poems cited in this chapter are listed, with page numbers, at the end of the chapter.

child started. Two poems that were written this way are "*When you're born you don't*" and "Where Will I Go."

Another way to create a climate conducive to the expression of fantasies is through music. Listening to records of instrumental music or to the sounds of animals, such as the recorded songs of whales, can help to free the flow of ideas (see "Copland's Jazz Concerto" and "Sounds Of The Whale").

Certain poems are particularly useful in evoking nighttime feelings —among them, "Sleeping With One Eye Open," "Moon Tiger," "The Bird Of Night," "Hands," and "*At night I hear an owl hooing.*" Asking young children a series of questions about going to bed, sleeping, and dreaming can move them towards a dreamlike frame of mind. Sometimes it helps to darken the room and whisper. Reproductions of paintings that suggest dreamscapes can be brought into the classroom. Pictures such as Magritte's *The Return,* Chagall's *Les Plumes en Fleurs*, and Rousseau's *The Sleeping Gypsy* may remind children of the quality of their own dreams.

They may discover that there can be a carry-over from home to school, that even one's worst dreams can be retrieved and articulated. In "*I hear a strange noise. Suddenly*" a fifth grader's nightmare is reported from start to finish, enhanced by use of the present tense and the breathless piling up of concrete detail. Older students may respond to "Pass/Fail," an adult nightmare about exams.

Once children know that they can make poems out of their fantasies and dreams, they may find the word "dream" a handy one to use when trying out an idea that otherwise seems too "crazy" to be acceptable (see "This Is My Dream" and "The Bad Children Dream"). Sometimes a child is able to move into the strange reality of dreams and then back out of it, thus acquiring power over both dream life and language, as in "Hard Wind."

See:

CHAPTER VI

PERSONA POEMS

A persona poem is a special kind of fantasy in which the writer becomes someone or something else: another person, an animal, a natural phenomenon, an object, a part of the body, an abstraction.

Putting on such masks appeals to many children. They enjoy the sensation of changing into another being—of being able to choose a voice suitable to their temperament or mood of the moment. Also, it is often relieving to say what you need to say in a disguised voice rather than to confront emotions directly.

Younger children who adopt a persona can become temporarily large and powerful or (as they sometimes wish to be) tinier and safer. For teen-agers, the persona poem provides a way for feelings to be revealed and concealed at the same time, and it offers an acceptable mode of voicing grievances.

In each metamorphosis the child is trying out a new way of being, speaking, looking and is stretching to find a concrete vocabulary suitable to the new persona.

When introducing the persona concept to students, a simple lead-in phrase such as "I wish I were a," "I am a," "If I were," "I don't want to be" may be sufficient to get a child started on a persona poem.

Or the idea of a conversation can be introduced—whether it is between two animals ("Fair Catch"), two objects ("Bleeding"), or between a person and some other thing ("Oh Tree").

Sometimes it is helpful to present a more tangible, visible device along with one or two model poems. Interesting objects can be brought into the classroom: fruits and vegetables, flowers, weeds, stones, shells, feathers, gloves, a necklace, a hat, string, a hammer, a spoon, a handmade bowl.

Being an Object

If you look at the world from the object's point of view, how would

For easy reference, all poems cited in this chapter are listed, with page numbers, at the end of the chapter.

it feel (see "Onion" and "A Pencil")? When you are the object, what do you see? Eat? What is your skin like? What do you love and what do you hate? How do you go to sleep and what do you dream about? What have you always wished for? Who are your friends? Enemies? Are you like the others? Do you have a special secret or knowledge or a particular way of speaking or singing (see "Mushrooms" and "I Am,")?

Some children will put every object in sight to these tests: wastebasket, chalkboard, shoes, lunch box, pencil sharpener. Others may launch into a barrage of complaints, prayers, and tales of revenge written from the viewpoints of mistreated or underrated objects. Others make boasts or confessions.

A familiar object, looked at from "the inside out," can tell a story or explore feelings (see "Stone" and "Ceiling"). Other evocative objects might be: an envelope, a door, mirror, window, tent, wheel, bridge, scissors, or a house.

Being a Natural Phenomenon

Many things that cannot be brought into the classroom can serve as provocative personae. Natural phenomena such as the moon, the sun, a star, a hurricane, an icicle, a waterfall, a mountain, or a volcano can become exciting masks to try on (see *"I am a sandune at"*).

Being a Part of the Body

It is easy to overlook the most readily available personae: parts of one's own body. The poet can become a hand, a mouth, an eye, a face, a wound, a teardrop.

Being an Abstraction

Some children test what it would be like to become an abstraction—preferably not Happiness, Peace or Pollution, which invite vague rhetoric, but perhaps a number, a day of the week, a color (see "Light Green" and "Protector").

Being an Animal

Children, and adults too, like to contemplate what it would be like to change into an animal, a bird, or an insect. The animal may be a real one, as familiar as your pet or as unusual as a giraffe or dinosaur, or it may be an invention. For example, in Donald Hall's "Self-Portrait, As A Bear," the poet becomes a fantastic animal—a foolish looking and endearing bear/bird/person (see also "The Magical Mouse" and "Bird-aggators Birdaggators").

30

Being Another Person

An adult poet who feels affinity for another person (perhaps an historical or mythological figure) may write a poem in the voice of that person. Some children write this way, too, or they enjoy becoming a cartoon or TV character, the President, a sibling, a person of the opposite sex.

Photographs, such as those from *The Family Of Man*, help to spark empathy in children and often act as catalysts for persona poems. The poet "enters" the landscape of the photograph and becomes the person in it: an old man, an angry child, a dreamy teen-ager. The notion of liberating someone's voice from its black-and-white silence is particularly appealing to students of junior high school age.

Some children, distancing themselves a bit, would rather take on the persona of an object in the photograph than that of a person: the fence, rather than the children behind it; the flute, rather than the player.

Because many children adopt the persona device as their own particular way of writing a poem, persona poems can appear no matter what the writing assignment. "A Pencil" was written in a session on acrostic poems. From workshops on dreams came "I Am An Egg" and "This Is My Dream." The sand dune poem was written during a session on shaped poems.

See:

CHAPTER VII

POEMS WRITTEN TO A "YOU"

Who do you feel like writing a poem to? Poetry is a communicative art; all poems are, in some sense, messages. Sometimes the poet is talking to himself or herself, sometimes to a universal reader who is addressed as "you," as in "Permit Me To Warn You." Often, though, the "you" in a poem is a particular person or a particular animal, object, or abstraction.

Message poems take many forms. Among them are poems written as directions, as warnings, as apologies or thanks, as invocations, or as prayers.

Directions and Warnings

Children, who so often are on the receiving end of warnings and directives, enjoy turning the tables and becoming the one who does the warning or who hands out the instructions. The tone of the poem will depend on the child's mood. Directions might be given for something one obviously already knows how to do (see "How To Sit") or for creating something familiar (such as a hat, knife, or cat) or for inventing something like a brand new color.

A list of directives can build up an imaginative, unified world. "To Paint The Portrait Of A Bird" shows how a fantastic story can be told through the device of giving instructions. In "Blue Cornucopia" an entire inventory of selected, favorite blue things hangs on the imperative word: "pick."

Warnings can be given to people, real or invented (as in "The Key To It All"), to animals (as in "Turkey"), to fruits and vegetables (as in *"Now listen, you watermelons"*), even to objects. In "Rattlesnake Ceremony Song" the rattler is kept at bay by the repeated warning, "Do

---

For easy reference, all poems cited in this chapter are listed, with page numbers, at the end of the chapter.

not touch me," a line children might like to make use of in their own poems.

Apologies and Thanks

A poem may apologize in all seriousness for damage done in the past ("First Deer"), for something that was actually a delightful experience ("This Is Just To Say"), or for dramatic effect when creating a joke ("Uh Oh").

Letters or notes of thanks can be addressed to God, to a friend or relative, or simply to "you." Addressing such an anonymous "you" sometimes enables children to express feelings they fear might not otherwise be acceptable.

Invocations and Prayers

Some poems are cries for help. One way to make this kind of message available to children is to suggest writing a secret message or a message in a bottle. Whether the results are serious or humorous, this concept is apt to hold great charm for certain students. Another way is to show children some model poems that are communications to the spirit world. "Darkness Song" speaks of the anxiety the dark brings and asks for help during the long night's journey. "Shaman's Incantation To Exorcise A Demon" invokes the aid of all natural and animal spirits on behalf of a sick man. Children enjoy reading this poem aloud and even acting it out. They might like to write their own incantations.

See:

CHAPTER VIII

HOW LONG SHOULD A POEM BE?

Unless the poet has chosen a form in which the number of lines is predetermined (e.g., a haiku, a sestina, an alphabet poem), each poem will tend to find its own best length. Whether the poem is long, short, or in between, when children reach the end of a poem they usually know it.

Longer Poems

Some writing pours out in a rush of words. In the urgency of the telling a kind of natural rhythm begins and then takes over, controlling what is to come next. When the urge is to tell a dream or a fantasy as quickly as possible, the writing is often breathless and intense. Two children's poems written this way are *"I hear a strange noise. Suddenly"* and *"When you're born you don't."* When the urge is to share some wonderful perception, even a young child's poem can be extremely lyrical, as in "Wind Has Come With The Birds."

This kind of spontaneous writing may result in an extended story or fantasy; sometimes it takes the form of a stream of consciousness. In either case the "gush" comes to an end when the energy behind it has expended itself.

Short Poems

A quick, intense observation; a brief, impassioned message; a swift flash of inspiration (sometimes funny)—any of these can produce a small poem that feels like a complete unit in itself. A small poem gives you the freedom to say something in a hurry and to stop as soon as you're through. There is no padding, no excess language. Given encouragement, some children will write a whole string of such poems, often trying out the same idea or form in a different way, like an artist doing a series of quick sketches.

For easy reference, all poems cited in this chapter are listed, with page numbers, at the end of the chapter.

Because it seems easy to teach a short form with "rules" and because the natural world provides convenient subject matter, many teachers gravitate toward the Japanese haiku. The formal requirements appear to be simple: a three-line, nonrhyming nature poem of 17 syllables. (Translated haiku sometimes have a few syllables more or less.) However, a successful haiku relies not only on syllable count, keen perceptions, and selection of appropriate details but also on some new insight based on wisdom and sophistication. This integral element of the haiku can hardly be expected of children.

Instead of teaching children to write this deceptively simple form, therefore, teachers might make better use of haiku by including them as models with other poems. The succinctness of the form provides an interesting contrast when presented with longer poems. For example, the haiku *"The temple bell stops,"* a poem that implies various kinds of echoes, might be included in a group of poems involving the sense of hearing (see Chapter IV).

See:

CHAPTER IX

LONGER FORMS FOR OLDER STUDENTS

Alphabet poems, sestinas, and multiple "ways of looking" are interesting forms to introduce to children who have had some experience in writing poems.

Alphabet Poems

Like acrostics, alphabet poems are poems with a "spine." Because they tend to be longer than acrostics and to provide a larger arena for word play, they appeal particularly to students at the junior high school level.

As a reading of the poems listed below will show, the alphabet—despite the apparent rigidity of its spine—can be manipulated in a number of interesting ways. For example, the order of the letters can be rearranged ("The Rate At Which Things Happen Where") or the alphabet can be made to go backwards (*"Z is a zerox machine"*).

For some poets the letters of the alphabet serve to stimulate the imagination. In the Hannigan poem, "A is a kite" directs attention to the kitelike shape of the letter A as well as to the indefinite article in "a kite." "Z is the sound they make when they sleep" reminds us of other kinds of associations with letters.

In "Clocktower" the sense of running out of time is reinforced by the closed, finite system of the alphabet. In the poem "And With The Sorrows Of This Joyousness" the alphabet is used to make a selective inventory. It begins with apparent random word play and, through a series of transformations, ends in the hope that by transforming the word you can transform the world.

See:

Sestinas

The sestina, an old French form (six stanzas of six lines each, followed by a three-line "envoy" stanza), provides some children with a sustained challenge. The six end-words of the lines in the first stanza must be repeated in the remaining stanzas in a certain pattern.* Within these confines, the poet has a good deal of room to navigate. No rhyme is required, only six end-words need be chosen, and the lines can be of any length.

A certain amount of flexibility in handling end-words helps to create excitement in the writing of a sestina. In "Homework Sestina," for example, the end-word *help* shifts to *helpless* in the fifth stanza and to *Help!* in the sixth. Similarly, *drag* becomes *drags, dragging* and, finally, *dragon.*

A sestina can bring together ideas, experiences, and feelings about a particular topic, as in "Music" or as in "Rink Keeper's Sestina: Hockey, hockey," which contrasts the brutality of today's professional hockey with the simple "black ice" hockey of the poet's memory.

The use of proper names (Zamboni, Phil Esposito, Boston Garden) helps to sustain reader interest in the hockey poem as well as in "Hallelujah: A Sestina," where names (Ebenezer, Daniel, John, James, Stone of Help, Robert) are an integral part of the poem's meaning.

See:

---

*

I	II	III	IV	V	VI	Envoy
1	6	3	5	4	2	2 & 5
2	1	6	3	5	4	4 & 3
3	5	4	2	1	6	6 & 1
4	2	1	6	3	5	
5	4	2	1	6	3	
6	3	5	4	2	1	

"Ways of Looking"

Wallace Stevens' poem "Thirteen Ways Of Looking At A Blackbird" demonstrates how a poet can capture in one place a number of different perspectives, attitudes and voices. It also provides a model for creating a montage from a group of small, partially related stanzas.

The blackbird can be seen from the distance, a tiny part of a larger landscape, as in the first and last stanzas. Or it can be viewed as a creature with the power to make ideas concrete, as in stanzas II, IV, VIII and IX. A small story (stanza XI) or direct speech (stanza VII) can also be incorporated in such an all-encompassing poem.

Additional ways of looking might include viewing an object as if through a magnifying glass; speaking to it; speaking in *its* voice; associating to its sound, smell, or color; observing it at different seasons or times of day (see "Fifteen Reflections On Volcanoes"). The device of building a poem in short stanzas out of a series of associations is used somewhat differently in "Twelve Ways Of Looking At The New York State Thruway From Syracuse To Boston."

See:

CHAPTER X

MORE CONNECTIONS

Good poems resist categorizing: the richer they are, and the more individual, the more difficult it is to "type" them. A single poem may serve as a model for a number of different ways to write poems.

In the preceding chapters, poems were grouped and regrouped to provide models for varying approaches to the writing of poetry. This chapter offers additional possible groupings: animals, city, conversations, family, feelings, food, inventories, living and dying, nature, night, places, school. Most of these groupings relate to subject matter; conversations and inventories, however, suggest new ways to organize poems.

Animals

How does it feel to be a giraffe, tall and voiceless? Both adults and children enjoy writing about animals, whether real ones (ordinary or unusual) or creatures of their own invention. The animals can be spoken to, described, empathized with, listed in a group with others; or the poet can "become" the animal in the poem.

City

Features of urban life appear naturally in the writing of city poets. There can be both positive and negative aspects, vibrancy and beauty as well as traffic, soot, and the fear associated with contemporary cities.

Conversations

In poems, anyone—animal, vegetable, or mineral—can take part in a conversation. In the poems listed below, conversations take place between 1) a person and an animal, 2) a person and a part of the body, 3) a person and a "piece" of nature, 4) two objects, 5) two animals.

Family

Brothers and sisters, parents, grandparents—the experience of living in a family, including both pleasant and unpleasant memories, is source material for poems.

Feelings

Older children occasionally confront their feelings directly and write poems entitled "Loneliness" or "Fear." Usually, though, genuine feelings are more likely to emerge in children's poems when the approach is more oblique. For example, many of the children's poems listed here were written during workshops on forms: shaped poems, acrostics, persona poems. A full repertoire of feelings emerges: delight, love, friendship, fear, hate, anxiety, loneliness, pride, shame, loss, resentment, yearning, wonder, awe.

43

Food

An interest in food can serve as the common denominator for children of mixed ages and backgrounds. In poems, naming foods helps to make remembered experience more vivid, and describing a favorite food (or a detested one) usually evokes strong feelings. The poet can speak in the voice of something that is ordinarily eaten (see "Onion"), can pretend that something inedible is tasty, can have food serve as a metaphor for something else (see "Mushrooms").

Inventories

The impulse to make inventories and lists—to be, like Walt Whitman, a "maker of catalogues"—surfaces in poets of all ages. An inventory can be a form of stock-taking, sometimes a highly personal one. It can be a selective enumeration of favorite items (trees, birds), or it can be more inclusive, a piling up of all the sounds in the room or of every manifestation of a color. A poem that incorporates a list may take unexpected turns; even a short list may have a surprise ending.

Living and Dying

Children are often concerned with questions about how they were born, how they'll die, how their lives fit into larger natural cycles. Their poems express concern with many aspects of what it means to be a human being.

45

Nature

The natural world continues to inspire poets. Some of the children's poems listed below make use of acrostic and shaped forms. Others are written from the point of view of a natural phenomenon such as a volcano, a waterfall, an echo, wave, or sand dune.

Night

The night—beautiful, mysterious, and often scary—is a provocative subject for poets of all ages.

Places

Thinking about and naming a place often serves to evoke feelings and memories. One place name can set in motion a whole train of recollections.

School

School is many things: a place, people, a way you feel, how you spend a good deal of your time. It tends to surface as a subject in almost any classroom poetry session and can remain a powerful theme for adult poets.

48

ANTHOLOGY

POEMS BY ADULTS

accidentally
broke a teacup—
reminds me
how good it feels
to break things

—Ishikawa Takuboku

AND WITH THE SORROWS OF THIS JOYOUSNESS

O apple into ant and beard
Into barn, clock into cake and dust
Into dog, egg into elephant and fingers
Into fields, geese into gramophones, and hills
Into houses, ice into isotopes and jugs
Into jaguars, kings into kindnesses and lanes
Into lattices, moons into meanwhiles and nears
Into nevers, orphans into otherwises and pegs
Into pillows, quarrels into quiets and races
Into rainbows, serpents into shores and thorns
Into thimbles, O unders into utmosts and vines
Into villages, webs into wholenesses and years
Into yieldings..O zeals of these unspeaking
And forever unsayable zones!

—Kenneth Patchen

.elApfelApfelApfel
.pfelApfelApfelApfelApfe
.elApfelApfelApfelApfelApfel
elApfelApfelApfelApfelApfelA
ApfelApfelApfelApfelApfelApfelA
ofelApfelApfelApfelApfelApfelAp
ApfelApfelApfelApfelApfelApfelAp
pfelApfelApfelApfelApfelApfelAp
ApfelApfelApfelApfelApfelApfelA
felApfelApfelApfelApfelApfelA
pfelApfelApfelApfelWurmApf
ApfelApfelApfelApfelApfel
ApfelApfelApfelApfelApf
felApfelApfelApfelAr
ApfelApfelApfe
elApfelAr

—Reinhard Döhl

THE BALLAD OF RED FOX

Yellow sun yellow
Sun yellow sun
When, oh, when
Will red fox run?

When the hollow horn shall sound,
When the hunter lifts his gun
And liberates the wicked hound,
Then, oh, then shall red fox run.

Yellow sun yellow
Sun yellow sun
Where, oh, where
Will red fox run?

Through meadows hot as sulphur,
Through forests cool as clay,
Through hedges crisp as morning
And grasses limp as day.

Yellow sky yellow
Sky yellow sky
How, oh, how
Will red fox die?

With a bullet in his belly,
A dagger in his eye,
And blood upon his red red brush
Shall red fox die.

—Melvin Walker La Follette

BETWEEN WALLS

the back wings
of the

hospital where
nothing

will grow lie
cinders

in which shine
the broken

pieces of a green
bottle

—William Carlos Williams

THE BIRD OF NIGHT

A shadow is floating through the moonlight.
Its wings don't make a sound.
Its claws are long, its beak is bright.
Its eyes try all the corners of the night.

It calls and calls: all the air swells and heaves
And washes up and down like water.
The ear that listens to the owl believes
In death. The bat beneath the eaves,

The mouse beside the stone are still as death.
The owl's air washes them like water.
The owl goes back and forth inside the night,
And the night holds its breath.

—Randall Jarrell

BLEEDING

Stop bleeding   said the knife.
I would if I could said the cut.
Stop bleeding   you make me messy with this blood.
I'm sorry said the cut.
Stop or   I will sink in farther said the knife.
Don't said the cut.
The   knife did not say it couldn't help it but
it   sank in farther.
If   only you didn't bleed said the knife I wouldn't
have   to do this.
I know   said the cut I bleed too easily I hate
that I   can't help it I wish I were a knife like
you and   didn't have to bleed.
Well   meanwhile stop bleeding will you said the knife.
Yes you   are a mess and sinking in deeper said the cut, I
will have   to stop.
Have you   stopped by now said the k· ife.
I've almost   stopped I think.
Why must you   bleed in the first place said the knife.
For the same   reason maybe that you must do what you
must do said   the cut.
I can't stand   bleeding said the knife and sank in farther.
I hate it too said   the cut I know it isn't you it's
me you're lucky to be   a knife you ought to be glad about that.
Too many cuts around   said the knife they're
messy I don't know how   they stand themselves.
They don't said the cut.
You're bleeding again.
No I've stopped said the cut see you are coming out now the
blood is drying it will rub off you'll be shiny again and clean.
If only cuts wouldn't bleed   so much said the knife coming
out a little.
But then knives might become dull said the cut.
Aren't you still bleeding a   little said the knife.
I hope not said the cut.
I feel you are just a little.
Maybe just a little but I can stop now.
I feel a little wetness still   said the knife sinking in a
little but then coming out a   little.
Just a little maybe just enough said the cut.
That's enough now stop now do   you feel better now said the knife.
I feel I have to bleed to   feel I think said the cut.
I don't I don't have to   feel said   the knife drying now
becoming shiny.

                              --May Swenson

                    57

BLUE CORNUCOPIA

Pick any blue   sky-blue   cerulean   azure
cornflower   periwinkle   blue-eyed grass
blue bowl   bluebell   pick lapis lazuli
blue pool   blue girl   blue Chinese vase
or pink-blue chicory alias ragged sailor
or sapphire   bluebottle fly   indigo bunting
blue dragonfly or devil's darning needle
blue-green   turquoise   peacock   blue spruce
blue verging on violet   the fringed gentian
gray-blue   blue bonfire smoke autumnal
haze   blue hill   blueberry   distance
and darker blue   storm-blue   blue goose
ink   ocean   ultramarine   pick winter
blue snow-shadows   ice   the blue star Vega.

—Robert Francis

CAPE ANN

O quick quick quick, quick hear the song-sparrow
Swamp-sparrow, fox-sparrow, vesper-sparrow
At dawn and dusk. Follow the dance
Of the goldfinch at noon. Leave to chance
The Blackburnian warbler, the shy one. Hail
With shrill whistle the note of the quail, the bob-white
Dodging by bay-bush. Follow the feet
Of the walker, the water-thrush. Follow the flight
Of the dancing arrow, the purple martin. Greet
In silence the bullbat. All are delectable. Sweet sweet sweet
But resign this land at the end, resign it
To its true owner, the tough one, the sea-gull.
The palaver is finished.

—T. S. Eliot

CLOCK

in the sun
   the schoolroom clock
      shines like lake water

      the hours
         are small black twigs
            swept back

         left far behind
            by the strokes
               of the swimmer

—Kinereth Gensler

CLOCKTOWER

A is Andrew.
B is the boy he will become.
C is the clock chiming the
Days and nights. It is too
Early to tell his
Fortune. Fortunately he is
Going to a place neither of us has
Heard of yet,
Judging from what we
Know now.
L is the love he will come to
Many times just when he thinks his
Number is up.
One of us is the
Prisoner
Quietly watching the
Running boy who tries to
Save us from the
Time that pursues
Us, unfairly.
V is the victory we share
When we build towers. An
eXample is this poem, found
Years from now by a boy named Andrew.
Z is zero, the time I have left.

—Nina Nyhart

THE COMPUTER'S FIRST CHRISTMAS CARD

jollymerry
hollyberry
jollyberry
merryholly
happyjolly
jollyjelly
jellybelly
bellymerry
hollyheppy
jollyMolly
marryJerry
merryHarry
hoppyBarry
heppyJarry
boppyheppy
berryjorry
jorryjolly
moppyjelly
Mollymerry
Jerryjolly
bellyboppy
jorryhoppy
hollymoppy
Barrymerry
Jarryhappy
happyboppy
boppyjolly
jollymerry
merrymerry
merrymerry
merryChris
ammerryasa
Chrismerry
asMERRYCHR
YSANTHEMUM

--Edwin Morgan

COUNTING-OUT RHYME

Silver bark of beech, and sallow
Bark of yellow birch and yellow
   Twig of willow.

Stripe of green in moosewood maple,
Color seen in leaf of apple,
   Bark of popple.

Wood of popple pale as moonbeam,
Wood of oak for yoke and barn-beam,
   Wood of hornbeam.

Silver bark of beech, and hollow
Stem of elder, tall and yellow
   Twig of willow.

          —Edna St. Vincent Millay

DARKNESS SONG

We wait in the darkness!
Come, all ye who listen,
Help in our night journey:
Now no sun is shining;
Now no star is glowing;
Come show us the pathway:
The night is not friendly;
She closes her eyelids;
The moon has forgot us,
We wait in the darkness!

—American Indian (Iroquois)

FAMILY

When you swim in the surf off Seal Rocks, and your family
Sits in the sand
Eating potato salad, and the undertow
Comes which takes you out away down
To loss of breath loss of play and the power of play
Holler, say
Help, help, help. Hello, they will say,
Come back here for some potato salad.

It is then that a seventeen year old cub
Cruising in a helicopter from Antigua,
A jackstraw expert speaking only Swedish,
And remote from this area as a camel, says
Look down there, there is somebody drowning.
And it is you. You say, yes, yes.
And he throws you a line.
This is what is called the brotherhood of man.

—Josephine Miles

FIRST DEER

I trailed
your guts
    a mile through snow
before my second bullet
    stopped it all.
Believe me now,
there was a boy
who fed butterflies sugar water
and kept hurt birds
in boxes in his room.

        —Joseph Bruchac

FIRST LESSON

This is a meditation:
a snake with legs,
a one-legged snake,
a snake with wings,
a one-winged snake,
a rat with sparks,
a fiery rat,
a rat that sings,
a star rat,
a horse that explodes,
an atomic horse,
a horse that melts,
an ice horse,
a bee that flies through concrete,
a pneumatic bee,
a bee that lifts buildings,
the world's strongest bee,
a tree that eats the noses off children,
a bad tree,
a tree that grows inward until it is a dot,
a hill of dots that eats lots of children
(you are not meditating).

—James Tate

Fortune
has its cookies to give out

which is a good thing

since it's been a long time since

that summer in Brooklyn
when they closed off the street
one hot day
and the

FIREMEN

turned on their hoses
and all the kids ran out in it

in the middle of the street

and there were

maybe a couple dozen of us

out there
with the water squirting up
to the

sky

and all over
us
there was maybe only six of us
kids altogether
running around in our
barefeet and birthday
suits
and I remember Molly but then
the firemen stopped squirting their hoses
all of a sudden and went
back in
their firehouse
and
started playing pinochle again
just as if nothing
had ever
happened
while I remember Molly
looked at me and

ran in

because I guess really we were the only ones there

—Lawrence Ferlinghetti

68

HALLELUJAH: A SESTINA

A wind's word, the Hebrew Hallelujah.
I wonder they never give it to a boy
(Hal for short) boy with wind-wild hair.
It means Praise God, as well it should since praise
Is what God's for. Why didn't they call my father
Hallelujah instead of Ebenezer?

Eben, of course, but christened Ebenezer,
Product of Nova Scotia (hallelujah).
Daniel, a country doctor, was his father
And my father his tenth and final boy.
A baby and last, he had a baby's praise:
Red petticoat, red cheeks, and crow-black hair.

A boy has little say about his hair
And little about a name like Ebenezer
Except that he can shorten either. Praise
God for that, for that shout Hallelujah.
Shout Hallelujah for everything a boy
Can be that is not his father or grandfather.

But then, before you know it, he is a father
Too and passing on his brand of hair
To one more perfectly defenseless boy,
Dubbing him John or James or Ebenezer
But never, so far as I know, Hallelujah,
As if God didn't need quite that much praise.

But what I'm coming to—Could I ever praise
My father half enough for being a father
Who let me be myself? Sing hallelujah.
Preacher he was with a prophet's head of hair
And what but a prophet's name was Ebenezer,
However little I guessed it as a boy?

Outlandish names of course are never a boy's
Choice. And it takes time to learn to praise.
Stone of Help is the meaning of Ebenezer.
Stone of Help—what fitter name for my father?
Always the Stone of Help however his hair
Might graduate from black to Hallelujah.

Such is the old drama of boy and father.
Praise from a grayhead now with thinning hair.
Sing Ebenezer, Robert, sing Hallelujah!

—Robert Francis

HANDS

I

When I fall asleep
my hands leave me.

They pick up pens
and draw creatures
with five feathers
on each wing.

The creatures multiply.
They say: "We are large
like your father's
hands."

They say: "We have
your mother's
knuckles."

I speak to them:
"If you are hands,
why don't you
touch?"

And the wings beat
the air, clapping.
They fly

high above elbows
and wrists.
They open windows
and leave

rooms.
They perch in treetops
and under bushes
biting

their nails. "Hands,"
I call them.
But it is fall

71

and all creatures
with wings
prepare to fly
South.

II

When I sleep
the shadows of my hands
come to me.

They are softer than feathers
and warm as creatures
who have been close
to the sun.

They say: "We are the giver,"
and tell of oranges
growing on trees.

They say: "We are the vessel,"
and tell of journeys
through water.

They say: "We are the cup."

And I stir in my sleep.
Hands pull triggers
and cut
trees. But

the shadows of my hands
tuck their heads
under wings
waiting
for morning,

when I will wake
braiding

three strands of hair
into one.

—Siv Cedering Fox

72

HOW EVERYTHING HAPPENS (Based on a study of the Wave)


```
                                        happen.
                                    to
                                  up
                          stacking
                              is
                    something
When nothing is happening


When it happens
              something
                        pulls
                            back
                                not
                                    to
                                      happen.



When                               has happened.
      pulling back        stacking up
                  happens


          has happened                            stacks up.
When it              something              nothing
                          pulls back while



Then nothing is happening.


                                  happens.
                                and
                          forward
                      pushes
                    up
                stacks
        something
Then
```

                                        --May Swenson

I look into a dragonfly's eye
and see
the mountains over my shoulder.

—Issa

IN THE LOBBY

In the lobby while people shook hands
and flashbulbs of friendship popped like smiles,
while you said hello and hello to everyone
who didn't matter and I stood stylishly by
pretending I didn't know you
suddenly
I took my machine gun and,
dressed as I was in maroon velvet,
mowed down the popular lecturer with
his witty charm and good wife,
his friends, clingers, all parasites
and passersthrough, all those related to me
by birth, marriage, and death,
until finally I could see the ceiling.

The walls were absolutely bare and solitary.
Across the tiled floor only you were left.
You smiled, took my arm, and we
began to go home together.

—Ruth Whitman

75

KNOXVILLE, TENNESSEE

I always like summer
best
you can eat fresh corn
from daddy's garden
and okra
and greens
and cabbage
and lots of
barbecue
and buttermilk
and homemade ice-cream
at the church picnic
and listen to
gospel music
outside
at the church
homecoming
and go to the mountains with
your grandmother
and go barefooted
and be warm
all the time
not only when you go to bed
and sleep

   —Nikki Giovanni

LISTENING TO GROWNUPS QUARRELING,

standing in the hall against the
wall with my little brother, blown
like leaves against the wall by their
voices, my head like a pingpong ball
between the paddles of their anger;
I knew what it meant
to tremble like a leaf.

Cold with their wrath, I heard
the claws of the rain
pounce. Floods
poured through the city,
skies clapped over me,
and I was shaken, shaken
like a mouse
between their jaws.

—Ruth Whitman

Loveliest of what I leave behind
    is the sunlight,
and loveliest after that the shining stars,
    and the moon's face,
but also cucumbers that are ripe,
    and pears, and apples.

        —Praxilla of Sicyon
         (translated by Richmond Lattimore)

LYING IN A HAMMOCK AT WILLIAM DUFFY'S FARM IN PINE ISLAND, MINNESOTA

Over my head I see the bronze butterfly,
Asleep on the black trunk,
Blowing like a leaf in green shadow.
Down the ravine behind the empty house,
The cowbells follow one another
Into the distances of the afternoon.
To my right,
In a field of sunlight between two pines,
The droppings of last year's horses
Blaze up into golden stones.
I lean back, as the evening darkens and comes on.
A chicken hawk floats over, looking for home.
I have wasted my life.

—James Wright

THE MAGICAL MOUSE

I am the magical mouse
I don't eat cheese
I eat sunsets
And the tops of trees

I don't wear fur

I wear funnels
Of lost ships and the weather
That's under dead leaves
I am the magical mouse

I don't fear cats

Or woodowls
I do as I please
Always
I don't eat crusts
I am the magical mouse
I eat
Little birds and maidens

That taste like dust

—Kenneth Patchen

MOON TIGER

The moon tiger.
In the room, here.
It came in, it is
prowling sleekly
under and over
the twin beds.
See its small head,
silver smooth,
hear the pad of its
large feet. Look,
its white stripes
in the light that slid
through the jalousies.
It is sniffing our
clothes, its cold nose
nudges our bodies.
The beds are narrow,
but I'm coming in with you.

—Denise Levertov

81

MUSHROOMS

Overnight, very
Whitely, discreetly,
Very quietly

Our toes, our noses
Take hold on the loam,
Acquire the air.

Nobody sees us,
Stops us, betrays us;
The small grains make room.

Soft fists insist on
Heaving the needles,
The leafy bedding,

Even the paving.
Our hammers, our rams,
Earless and eyeless,

Perfectly voiceless,
Widen the crannies,
Shoulder through holes. We

Diet on water,
On crumbs of shadow,
Bland-mannered, asking

Little or nothing.
So many of us!
So many of us!

We are shelves, we are
Tables, we are meek,
We are edible,

Nudgers and shovers
In spite of ourselves.
Our kind multiplies:

We shall by morning
Inherit the earth.
Our foot's in the door.

—Sylvia Plath

Now listen, you watermelons—
if any thieves come—
turn into frogs!

—Issa

OLD FLORIST

That hump of a man bunching chrysanthemums
Or pinching-back asters, or planting azaleas,
Tamping and stamping dirt into pots,—
How he could flick and pick
Rotten leaves or yellowy petals,
Or scoop out a weed close to flourishing roots,
Or make the dust buzz with a light spray,
Or drown a bug in one spit of tobacco juice,
Or fan life into wilted sweet-peas with his hat,
Or stand all night watering roses, his feet blue in rubber boots.

—Theodore Roethke

PASS/FAIL

"Examination dreams are reported to persist even
into old age..."
                                 Time magazine

You will never graduate
from this dream
of blue books.
No matter how
you succeed awake,
asleep there is a test
waiting to be failed.
The dream beckons
with two dull pencils,
but you haven't even
taken the course;
when you reach for a book—
it closes a door
in your face; when
you conjugate a verb—
it is in the wrong
language.
Now the pillow becomes
a blank page. Turn it
to the cool side;
you will still smother
in all of the feathers
that have to be learned
by heart.

                        —Linda Pastan

PERMIT ME TO WARN YOU

Permit me to warn you
against this automobile rushing to embrace you
with outstretched fender

—Charles Reznikoff

POEM

I loved my friend.
He went away from me.
There is nothing more to say.
The poem ends,
Soft as it began—
I loved my friend.

—Langston Hughes

POMANDER

pomander
open pomander
open poem and her
open poem and him
hymn and hymen leander
high man pen meander
o pen poem me and her
pen me poem me and him
om mane padme hum
pad me home panda hand
open up o holy panhandler
ample panda pen or bamboo pond
ponder a bonny poem pomander opener
open banned peon penman hum and banter
open hymn and pompom band and panda hamper
o i am a pen open man or happener
i am open manner happener
happy are we open
poem and a pom
poem and a panda
poem and aplomb

—Edwin Morgan

THE PORTRAIT

My mother never forgave my father
for killing himself,
especially at such an awkward time
and in a public park,
that spring
when I was waiting to be born.
She locked his name
in her deepest cabinet
and would not let him out,
though I could hear him thumping.
When I came down from the attic
with the pastel portrait in my hand
of a long-lipped stranger
with a brave moustache
and deep brown level eyes,
she ripped it into shreds
without a single word
and slapped me hard.
In my sixty-fourth year
I can feel my cheek
still burning.

—Stanley Kunitz

THE RATE AT WHICH THINGS HAPPEN WHERE

A is a kite.
B is the boy running with
W is with the kite
C is a crow in a tree
L is the crow's laughing at
F is the flight the crow's laughing at
K is what the crow knows
O is a sense of order and
D is the boy's design to
G is get married some day
T is what is true and
X is what we know
H is the end of the crow in this poem
S is the season, Spring of the
Y is the year
J is Janet. He will marry Janet.
R is the rest of this poem
Q is the question of meaning
M is Mnemosyne who remembers Peter
P is Peter who flew a kite and married Janet
E is everything else but this poem
Z is the sound they make when they sleep
V is in their very warm bed
N is near each other under
U is under the covers at night.

—Paul Hannigan

RATTLESNAKE CEREMONY SONG

The king snake said to the rattlesnake:
Do not touch me!
You can do nothing with me.
Lying with your belly full,
Rattlesnake of the rock pile,
Do not touch me!
There is nothing you can do,
You rattlesnake with your belly full,
Lying where the ground-squirrel holes are thick.
Do not touch me!
What can you do to me?
Rattlesnake in the tree clump,
Stretched in the shade,
You can do nothing;
Do not touch me!
Rattlesnake of the plains,
You whose white eye
The sun shines on,
Do not touch me!

—American Indian
(Translated by A.L. Kroeber)

RINK KEEPER'S SESTINA: Hockey, hockey

Call me Zamboni. Nights my job is hockey.
I make the ice and watch the kids take slapshots
At each other. They act like Esposito,
As tough in the slot as Phil, as wild with fury
In fights. Their coaches tell me this is pleasure.
But it isn't pleasure. What it is, is Hockey.

Now let me tell you what I mean by Hockey.
I mean the fights. I mean young kids in fury,
And all these coaches yelling for more slapshots.
I tell you, blood is spilled here. This is pleasure?
It seems to me the coaches should teach hockey,
Not how to act like Schultz or Esposito.

Look, I have nothing against Phil Esposito.
He's one of the greats, no question, it's a pleasure
To watch him play. My point is, why teach fury?
If I know life (at least if I know hockey),
Then fury's here to stay. We don't need Hockey
To tell us that, we don't need fights and slapshots.

Like yesterday. I heard a coach yell, "Slapshots!
Take slapshots, son! You think Phil Esposito
Hangs back? And hit! And hit again! That's hockey!"
But he was wrong. The kid was ten. That's Hockey.
You could tell the boy admired his coach's fury.
It won't be long before he hits with pleasure.

Sure, I'm no saint. I know. I've gotten pleasure
From fury, too, like any man. And hockey
At times gets changed around in me to Hockey.
I've yelled for blood at Boston Garden. Slapshots?
They've thrilled me. I've seen men clobber Esposito
And loved it when he hit them back with fury.

But you know what? Before these days of fury,
When indoor rinks were just a gleam in Hockey
Fanatics' eyes, there was no greater pleasure
Than winter mornings. Black ice. (Esposito
Knew days like this as a boy.) Some friends. No slapshots,
But a clear, cold sky. Choose teams. Drop the puck. Play hockey.

Yes, before big Hockey (sorry, Esposito),
Before the fury and all the blazing slapshots,
We had great pleasure outdoors playing hockey.

                              —George Draper

SAM'S WORLD

sam's mother has
grey combed hair

she will never touch
it with a hot iron

she leaves it
the way the lord
intended

she wears it proudly
a black and grey
round head of hair

—Sam Cornish

SEA-WASH

The sea-wash never ends.
The sea-wash repeats, repeats.
Only old songs? Is that all the sea knows?
    Only the old strong songs?
    Is that all?
The sea-wash repeats, repeats.

—Carl Sandburg

SELF-PORTRAIT, AS A BEAR

Here is a fat animal, a bear
that is partly a dodo.
Ridiculous wings hang at his shoulders
while he plods in the brickyards
at the edge of the city, smiling
and eating flowers. He eats them
because he loves them
because they are beautiful
because they love him.
It is eating flowers which makes him fat.
He carries his huge stomach
over the gutters of damp leaves
in the parking lots in October,
but inside that paunch
he knows there are fields of lupine
and meadows of mustard and poppy.
He encloses sunshine.
Winds bend the flowers
in combers across the valley,
birds hang on the stiff wind,
at night there are showers, and the sun
lifts through a haze every morning
of the summer in the stomach.

—Donald Hall

SHAMAN'S INCANTATION TO EXORCISE A DEMON

Spirit spirit
lord of this place
flame in the center
father of our world
with your eight winds
eight corners of our world
draw near us now
help us

spirit spirit
lord of grasses
father of trees
all these your tassels
your feathers
rise up now
help us

Sea Mother
mother of seven
mounds of snow
these seven snow mounds
your seven blankets
come up now
draw near

with your collar
of black foxes
circling around
with your foam
of white foxes
leaping leaping
with your waves
of cub foxes
standing up
on hind paws
rise up now
help us

Light
Creator
Grandfather
you with three bridles
come

free us from
the invisible one
the one who tears
and tears

with your inner heat
Flame Father
draw near now
stand

if a storm swirls
around my tent
let me stand
firm

if a storm comes
up around my tent
may my inner poles
hold firm

listen
I'm a shaman
spirits rise for me
draw near me now
animal spirits
rise up now
help me

diver comes
ga ga ga
snipe comes up
cok cok cok cok
with his two great brothers
turri turri
kurr kurr
eagle comes
pil pil pil
stork comes up
kinirik kinirik
wolf comes
ooooooooooooooooooooooo
bear comes up
goo goo goo

ga ga ga
cok cok cok cok
turri turri turri
kurr kurr kurr kurr
pil pil
kinirik kinirik
oooooooooooooooo ooooooooooooooo
goo goo goo goo
oooooooooooooooooooooooo

animal spirits
come round me now
draw near me now
stand

listen you
invisible one
my scream's a storm
covering this world
leave this man
this sick one here
leave this man
alone

your invisible place
calls you calls you
go

Light
Creator
Grandfather
let that invisible
one drown
let him fall
through the earth
eating mouthfuls of dirt
let him drown
down there
below

Light
Creator
Grandfather
you with three bridles
come

with your light
your breath
raise our sick friend
may our friend rise up
now breathe

     —Yukaghir shaman song
      (adaptation by David Cloutier)

SIMULTANEOUSLY

Simultaneously, five thousand miles apart,
two telephone poles, shaking and roaring
and hissing gas, rose from their emplacements
straight up, leveled off and headed
for each other's land, alerted radar
and ground defense, passed each other
in midair, escorted by worried planes,
and plunged into each other's place,
steaming and silent and standing straight,
sprouting leaves.

—David Ignatow

SKINNY POEM

Skinny
poem,
all
your
ribs
showing
even
without
a
deep
breath

thin
legs
rotted
with
disease.

Live
here!
on
this
page,
barely
making it,
like

the
mass
of
mankind.

—Lou Lipsitz

SLEEPING WITH ONE EYE OPEN

Unmoved by what the wind does,
The windows
Are not rattled, nor do the various
Areas
Of the house make their usual racket—
Creak at
The joints, trusses, and studs.
Instead,
They are still. And the maples,
Able
At times to raise havoc,
Evoke
Not a sound from their branches'
Clutches.
It's my night to be rattled,
Saddled with spooks. Even the half moon
(Half man,
Half dark), on the horizon,
Lies on
Its side, casting a fishy light,
Which alights
On my floor, lavishly lording
Its morbid
Look over me. Oh, I feel dead,
Folded
Away in my blankets for good, and
Forgotten.
My room is clammy and cold,
Moonhandled
And weird. The shivers
Wash over
Me, shaking my bones, my loose ends
Loosen,
And I lie sleeping with one eye open,
Hoping
That nothing, nothing will happen.

—Mark Strand

104

STONE

Go inside a stone
That would be my way.
Let somebody else become a dove
Or gnash with a tiger's tooth.
I am happy to be a stone.

From the outside the stone is a riddle:
No one knows how to answer it.
Yet within, it must be cool and quiet
Even though a cow steps on it full weight,
Even though a child throws it in a river;
The stone sinks, slow, unperturbed
To the river bottom
Where the fishes come to knock on it
And listen.

I have seen sparks fly out
When two stones are rubbed,
So perhaps it is not dark inside after all;
Perhaps there is a moon shining
From somewhere, as though behind a hill—
Just enough light to make out
The strange writings, the star-charts
On the inner walls.

—Charles Simic

The temple bell stops—
  but the sound keeps coming
  out of the flowers.

—Basho

THIRTEEN WAYS OF LOOKING AT A BLACKBIRD

I

Among twenty snowy mountains
The only moving thing
Was the eye of the blackbird.

II

I was of three minds,
Like a tree
In which there are three blackbirds.

III

The blackbird whirled in the autumn winds.
It was a small part of the pantomime.

IV

A man and a woman
Are one.
A man and a woman and a blackbird
Are one.

V

I do not know which to prefer,
The beauty of inflections
Or the beauty of innuendoes,
The blackbird whistling
Or just after.

VI

Icicles filled the long window
With barbaric glass.
The shadow of the blackbird
Crossed it, to and fro.
The mood
Traced in the shadow
An indecipherable cause.

VII

O thin men of Haddam
Why do you imagine golden birds?
Do you not see how the blackbird
Walks around the feet
Of the women about you?

VIII

I know noble accents
And lucid, inescapable rhythms;
But I know, too,
That the blackbird is involved
In what I know.

IX

When the blackbird flew out of sight,
It marked the edge
Of one of many circles.

X

At the sight of blackbirds
Flying in a green light,
Even the bawds of euphony
Would cry out sharply.

XI

He rode over Connecticut
In a glass coach.
Once, a fear pierced him,
In that he mistook
The shadow of his equipage
For blackbirds.

XII

The river is moving.
The blackbird must be flying.

XIII

It was evening all afternoon.
It was snowing
And it was going to snow.
The blackbird sat
In the cedar-limbs.

—Wallace Stevens

THIS IS JUST TO SAY

I have eaten
the plums
that were in
the icebox

and which
you were probably
saving
for breakfast

Forgive me
they were delicious
so sweet
and so cold

—William Carlos Williams

TO PAINT THE PORTRAIT OF A BIRD

Paint first a cage
with an open door
paint then
something pretty
something simple
something handsome
something useful
for the bird
then place the canvas against a tree
in a garden
in a wood
or in a forest
hide behind the tree
silently
motionless
Sometimes the bird arrives at once
but it may also take many years
before making up its mind
Do not be discouraged
wait
wait if need be many years
a speedy or a delayed arrival
bears no relation
to the success of the portrait
When the bird arrives
if it arrives
observe the most profound silence
wait until the bird enters the cage
and when it has entered
close the door gently with a stroke of a brush
then

paint out one by one all the bars of the cage
taking care to touch none of the bird's feathers
Paint then the portrait of a tree
choosing the loveliest of its branches
for the bird
paint too the green foliage and the fresh wind
the dust of the sun
and the noise of insects in the grass in the summer heat
and then wait for the bird to sing
If the bird does not sing
it is a bad sign
a sign that the picture is bad
but if it sings it is a good sign
a sign that you can sign
So you pluck gently then
one of the bird's feathers
and you write your name in a corner of the portrait.

—Jacques Prévert
(translated by John Dixon Hunt)

TO THE HAND

What the eye sees is a dream of sight
what it wakes to
is a dream of sight

and in the dream
for every real lock
there is only one real key
and it's in some other dream
now invisible

it's the key to the one real door
it opens the water and the sky both at once
it's already in the downward river
with my hand on it
my real hand

and I am saying to the hand
turn

open the river

—W. S. Merwin

TRAIN TUNE

Back through clouds
Back through clearing
Back through distance
Back through silence

Back through groves
Back through garlands
Back by rivers
Back below mountains

Back through lightning
Back through cities
Back through stars
Back through hours

Back through plains
Back through flowers
Back through birds
Back through rain

Back through smoke
Back through noon
Back along love
Back through midnight

—Louise Bogan

WE REAL COOL

The Pool Players.
Seven at the Golden Shovel.

We real cool. We
Left school. We

Lurk late. We
Strike straight. We

Sing sin. We
Thin gin. We

Jazz June. We
Die soon.

—Gwendolyn Brooks

POEMS
BY CHILDREN

At night   I hear an owl   hooing
      like   this   hoo   hoo
and tigers growling.
I hear the moon
      talking to the sun.

—Jon Eisenthal, 2nd grade

THE BAD CHILDREN DREAM

The children that were never good
saw in a dream grass blowing
and lives flying away.

—Paul Arsenault, 4th grade

THE BASEBALL DREAM

the game is almost over
9 to 6 we're losing last
of the ninth bases loaded
I'm up the pitch is foul ball
one strike the pitch is ball one
then next ball two the next
pitch was a strike then another ball
full count the pitch is home run
and when the game was over
I got the game ball

—Matthew John Connelly, 4th grade

BICYCLE

Balancing on my bicycle
I can ride freely wherever I wish
Cool winds blowing in my face
Later, I launch down the hill
Eating my way through time

—Debbie Wien, 7th grade

BIKES

Bikes have two wheels,
a seat, a handlebar.
And pedals and then
someone to ride it.

—Peter K., 2nd grade

BIRDAGGATORS   BIRDAGGATORS

Birdaggators love to swing in mud,
They love to swallow snakes.
They love to sway down the river.
Birdaggators lie in the sun.
They eat their own babies.
Birdaggators   Birdaggators
They look like a bird and a
allaggator   allaggator
have a long nose and big eyes.
They have long wings and feet
they have an allaggator's tail and teeth.
They are the best looking animals I've
                  seen.

I know   I am one.

—Anthony Bonina and Wayne Gazaille, 5th grade

CEILING

I would like to be a ceiling
where I could watch them,
and know how they're all feeling,
My family that is,
the floors and the walls,
Sometimes I dream
that we all have a fall,
When people move in they stick
things and hang things and change
the floors,
It makes me cry really hard
to see my family change
makes me really sad

—Anonymous, 5th grade

THE CELLAR

I love my queer cellar with its dusty smell,
Its misty smell like smoke-fringes
From clouds blowing past;
With its shelves of jams and cookies,
With its boxes...barrels...
Woodpiles here and there.
There is a passageway
To an unknown room
Where bins hold carrots and things.
There are glass doors that bang
And cobweb windows.
I love the quietness of my cellar
Thinking in the dark,
My cellar has apples in its breath,
Potatoes even,
That smell of earth.

—Hilda Conkling

Clap clop
popcorn
nose house
flay fly flew
new noise no
snap snip snop
clip clup cluzz
clep stop me

—Chip Hughes, 2nd grade

THE CLASS OF POEMS

First noise,
Then silence.
The thinking,
Writing,
Conversing.
Sharing their feelings
With everyone around.
Wondering if
Their poem is good enough,
Or has enough feeling,
So it could be read to the class.
But nothing has to be perfect.
It's the way the person himself
Feels. It doesn't matter how
Anyone else thinks about it.
The author, and the author alone,
Only knows the right feelings,
For the poem.

—Patricia G. Karidoyanes, 9th grade

COLORADO

Crammed in the city
Or stuck in the traffic
Living like a cockroach
Over the country I fly
Reaching higher to touch the sun
Arriving in
Dear Denver
Open life

—Lois P. Brody, 8th grade

128

COPLAND'S JAZZ CONCERTO

It makes me think of the king
and queen and they dance. But
the queen did not want to dance.
So she balleted instead. And she
keeps on dancing and never stops
and the king comes and says
please dance with me and she said
YES! And they danced. And then
the princess came in and danced with
the king. And the queen says stop!
But they dance jazz! And she does
the jazz! and she gets killed!
And the king and queen dance and
dance.

—Florence B., 4th grade

CRAIG

Chaotically savoir faire
Radical at heart
Ambitiously oriented
Idiosyncrasies abundant
Gallant gentleman

—Craig Medoff, 8th grade

Dark purple
gloomy purple
shady purple
dim purple
shadowy purple
lightless purple
light of the un purple
brilliant purple
bright purple
vividness purple
radiant purple
luminous purple
blazing purple
glaring purple
glittering purple
Dark of the un purple
    EVERYTHING PURPLE
    purple

    —Gordon Bennett, 8th grade

DOG TALK

Oh Oh nooooo
Here comes
that girl she is going
to pick me up squeeze
me and then she's
going to say, "Oh poocheee
baby, I missed you."
She's going to pick
me up hug me and
then the doorbell
will ring
and she'll drop
me crunch
thud oooff
And I'll think
now's my chance
but she'll go, "Oh,
just the mailman."
Every day this happens.

—Gregory Petrini, 4th grade

DRIFTING

Flying to the
moon. Even Mars
if I want to. Then
to the bottom
of the sea. Up to
the stars. And even
into me.

—Tim H., 4th grade

DRIP, DRIP

A
dr
op o
f w
ater
fal
li
ng
int
o a
pon
d,
splash!

—Bruce Zohn, 8th grade

FAIR CATCH

Oh blackbird, blackbird
       What do you eat?
Eagle Eye, Eagle Eye, grapes
taste so fine.
Oh blackbird, blackbird, why eat fruit?
Eagle Eye, Eagle Eye, what do
you eat?
Oh blackbird, blackbird, I eat
       you!

—Richard Savage Jr., 7th grade

FEAR

Following a child
Every time Fear visits,
Afternoon or night, he says
Run, go ahead, I always catch up.

—R. F. Hannan, 7th grade

FIFTEEN REFLECTIONS ON VOLCANOES

I
Out of all the quiet mountains,
All the silent giants,
Only one speaks

II
A thousand gallant steeds,
Over a wooden bridge

III
An orchestra of slide whistles,
Tuning for an unknown symphony.

IV
A million black genies
Billowing in the wind

V
Oil and tomato soup
Bubbling in a black bowl.

VI
The blood of the earth, pours forth
From an open wound

VII
A lush tropical island...
Suddenly a hot black desert.

VIII
Coloring the sunset,
Like a child let loose with a paint box.

IX

A hundred mighty rivers,
Transformed into steam,
Are soon gone

X

And tell me, what is it
that you object so violently to?

XI

Ageless mountains
Sinking slowly into the sea,
Cry out, at the young upstart.

XII

The baby was throwing little stones,
And boulders

XIII

Tired of its old surroundings,
The fickle child, changes them every day.

XIV

When Mt. Vesuvius let down her hair
She smothered her loved ones,
In her fiery tresses.

XV

Oh mighty men... RUN!!!

—Pamela Burnley, 9th grade

138

GOING, GOING, GONE

Buildings flashing by
tables, lamps piled up.
Tied to the roof with taut rope,
leaving nothing.
My father drove to the tune
of a slamming door.
Slamming the door to the past.
No feelings in me.
Where was the past?
She stood, tall and stucco,
red, green, yellow, orange leaves,
like razors they scrape briefly over
    the sidewalk.
The world is a maze of doors.
And even today I am still ringing
    bells.

—Amy Sallen, 8th grade

HARD WIND

And the wind is blowing,
So hard that our neighbor's house has blown down.
Now our other neighbor's.
Now the one across the street.
A fire bird tells me that everyone is dead,

Everyone but my relatives.

No one is dead.

—Sarit Catz, 4th grade

HOMEWORK SESTINA

Homework
is a drag!
You can never get away from school.
We protest to the teachers
that we want more time for fun,
but it doesn't help.

We want help
with our homework
and we want homework to be fun.
But the work drags
on and teachers
still teach school.

If I forget my schoolbooks,
I'll need plenty of help,
but I know the teacher
won't sympathize much. At home
my dog starts to drag
my sock. She wants some fun

like I do. Funny,
she can play; she doesn't have school
to drag
her down. It helps
to have her sympathize with my homework.
I wish the teacher

did too, but teachers
do not assign fun.
When I'm at home
I'm at school.
I'm helpless!
This work is dragging

me down. Like a dragon,
the teacher
melts my free time more and more as I get older. Help!
This isn't funny.
School should be school
and home should be home.

—Andrew N., 6th grade

How do you feel, said the shell.
I feel like I have claustrophobia, the peanut said.
You must feel terrible inside there.
I do, said the peanut.
But not me, I feel wonderful
outside, it's too bad you weren't
like me, the outside type.
Well, I can't change what I am, said the peanut.

—Marianne D'Orsi, 7th grade

HOW TO SIT

If you don't know how to sit I'll teach you.
First you get a chair and a 10000 foot building.
You climb the building all the way and jump on the
chair. If you get hurt the xrays are on me. If that
does not work you turn the chair upside down and
drop it. Of Course all you will get will be such a
headache. If you climb up a pole with a chair
beside it and slide down you will be sitting.

And you owe me 100000000 dollars for giving you
lessons on how to sit.

—Anthony Bonina, 5th grade

I AM,

so small and green and fresh
It is cozy and warm
under the deep earth where I live
But I will soon grow—if
you take good care of me—I love
the feeling of the
water on my almost broken
skin I push and come
slowly at first out of the earth
then I look around
But it is not a forest, I see
cracks in the sidewalk

—Lois P. Brody, 8th grade

I am a
Sand une at
the beach where
the waves pound on me
and steal my sand away

I am a wave at the beach
I steal sand from the
Dunes very fast and
I carry it away
very far away.

—Pamela Burnley, 8th grade

146

I AM AN EGG

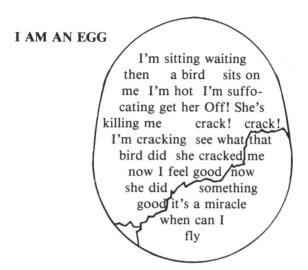

I'm sitting waiting
then a bird sits on
me I'm hot I'm suffo-
cating get her Off! She's
killing me crack! crack!
I'm cracking see what that
bird did she cracked me
now I feel good now
she did something
good it's a miracle
when can I
fly

—Stephen Cavanaugh, 4th grade

147

I am the tallest woman in the world
I am even taller than the
Empire State Building I can reach
the sky or a plane in the sky
I can touch a bird I can fly
that's a lie

—Cheri S., 3rd grade

I HATE MY CRIB

My brother
    kicked me
    out of my
    crib.

        Jay did it.

           —Kris Tibbert, 2nd grade

I HEAR:

talking, reading, compliments,
spelling problems. War poems,
mountain poems, ant poems,
laughing, paper rustling,
asking questions. Poems
whispering weirdness.

—Danny A. Sobel, 4th grade

I hear a strange noise. Suddenly
the whole town of Milford is on fire.
Millions of people are killed. I'm
running. Into the town of Franklin.
I look way down from the hill.
I see the town of Milford on fire.
I'm out of breath from running.
I cannot find my family. I'm starting
to cry because I cannot find them.
I find my Mother but I can't find
my father, my three brothers and my
two sisters.

                    when I woke up
Then I wake up and I'm shivering and
I go over to my father and ask him
if I can sleep with him the rest of
the night.
                    This is a true dream.

                        —Anthony Bonina, 5th grade

I KNOW A PLACE

I know a place with
streams and lakes running free
I know a place with deer running wild.
I also know a place dark with soot.

—Peter MacIntyre, 7th grade

I like mountains.
I like numbers.
I like letters.
I like Marc.

—David, 2nd grade

I was walking
down the street
when I noticed
some pretty
feet
legs
thighs
hips
lips
face

—Daryl H. Smith, 8th grade

It
melts
across
the sky
like the
drops in
the rain
yes yes
that's a
good name
the milkyway
that's what
it's called
the great
long milkyway
the chocolate
milkmilk
across the
sky yumm
yumm yumm
yumm yumm

—Daniel H., 4th grade

155

K is for knob on a door to open
E is for everything a boy and girl want
Y is for yearning, mysterious and dark

—Nell Swoish, 8th grade

THE KEY TO IT ALL

Batman—watch out!
They're burgling the city,
Using G-trills as
        weapons,
Holding the locksmith
        hostage in the
        back of an old
        piano
Batman—watch out!

—Miriam Lahage, 8th grade

Left out of all the little intimate conversations
Off in your own little dreams
Nobody to tell secrets to.
Living in lonely dreams
Impregnable fortresses.
Nasty shadows
Elusive people
Simple thing
Sunflowers

—Catherine Miller, 8th grade

LIGHT GREEN

Light green is ugly I hate it I
hate it. All the colors do:
regular green, pink, orange,
purple, red, blue, black.
If you see light green step on it.

—Anthony Bonina, 5th grade

MAINE

When the dark clouds above the sea
rise above the sun, every light
    turns off.

—L. M. Goetzl, 2nd grade

MATHEMATICS

hem a mat
tic, tic, tic
them acrobatics
tic, tic, tic
robots, lunatics
parties, really sick
keep in time, tic, tic, tic
pick a tune, trick or treat
tricky theorems, oh,
so
yick!
yick!
yick!

—Janet W., 8th grade

me beside the door
and trees and bushes too
the door was locked
and I knocked and
    knocked

—Patrick Motes, 4th grade

MIRROR

I was living in the mirror.
The small mirror
swallowed a big house.
Everybody will be swallowed
by the mirror
if they're standing near it.
Everybody is swallowed.
Children,
grownups,
everybody comes in one by one.
It never becomes crowded.
I lived in the mirror forever.

—Itozakura Takako, age 8

MIRROR

I used to think a mirror
was a liar, trying to make
me believe that I was a witch.
But I never believed it.

—Janet W., 8th grade

MUD

My father was never allowed to get dirty.
Underneath he wasn't ever a little boy
Dad, when will you be born?

—Aimee Rosen, 8th grade

MUSIC

The running sound of music
pours over me, like teardrops
pour over my face. It's like magic
how wonderful and foolish
I feel when I hear the freedom
of chords run to me over my mountain

of sadness. This tall grumpy mountain
was made when I wasn't allowed to hear my music.
When I don't hear it, I'm not free
to let myself feel. I can't laugh, or let tears
fall. But I feel like a fool
crying, especially when the magic

of music is not magical
anymore, when I can't hear it over my mountain
of foolish
hate and crying. The glorious music,
when I pause to hear it, takes away the tears
and I once again am free

from my hate. This freedom
is not really magical
because once I can see through my teardrops
the mountain
of not-seeing-clearly is gone. The music
is really crazily foolish

the way it helps me. Then it isn't foolish
because it helps me to free
myself from the hate and hear music,
be it real or not. This magic
of hearing music all the time is due to the mountain
disappearing when my tears do.

The teardrops
leave when my foolish
fears and hates decide to leave me for the mountain
where all hates and fears go. I am free
to listen to magical
wonderful, imaginative music.

My tears leave. I am free
to dream my foolish dreams, and let the magic
calm the mountain of hate, while I listen to music.

—Amrita Daniere, 8th grade

OH TREE

Oh tree, oh tree, how does it feel
to be blown in the wind,
oh tree, oh tree, how does it feel
to have birds light on your leaves?
Oh person, oh person, it feels just great
to have them land on me,
and the wind makes me feel free.

—Russell Reynolds, 4th grade

ONION

clear
colorless
circle
a ring
of
smell
my
skin
tanned
and
lined
my hair
straight
and light
my
inner
body
filled
with
thoughts
and then
my inner core
my heat
my heart
my tear

—Tirzah Lea Nardone, 7th grade

PANTHER

Black
as night
lithe
as cat
silhouetted
against
the moon,
it stalks,
    eyes
of jade,
    teeth
as spikes,
    talons
as blades
pouncing,
it strikes.
It rips the
fleet cheetah,
decapitates
its head.

—Hannibal King, 7th grade

A PENCIL

Please
everyone
never break
cut me
I write
Lovely don't break me

—David Gerbick, 5th grade

A PERSONAL INVENTORY

My mom says I am 14
I disagree with her
I believe in reincarnation
I think
I'm too old
There are 7 in my family
I like the color
gray best
horsebackriding is
my favorite sport.
I like the Beatles music best
I play piano
saxaphone and recorder
I never danced before
because I'm scared of
making a fool of myself
My favorite author is
James Foreman
I get depressed easily
and I love the
word *definitely*
and my 9 year old brother.
I would like to be an
architect
but I'm flunking Algebra
I like expressing myself
through art.
I enjoy singing
I never get enough sleep
and
I get too
involved with my friends
so they never have time
to be
themselves.
I don't act
like
Francesca Nasjleti

—Francesca Jo Nasjleti, 9th grade

PROTECTOR

I am large and sprawling,
tall and short, violent, famous,
the long gridiron pores in my
skin hold you in your vehicles
I see the dawn come and darkness
go. I am beautiful in my ugliness,
exciting. I am your protector—my
bridges are life lines.
I am a city.

—Christopher Dean, 8th grade

Rain sounds like machine guns
ddddddddddddddddddddddddd

—Charlie Marks, 2nd grade

Sensual
Exciting
X-rated

—Gordon Bennett, 8th grade

SIPPING ICE CREAM

soft spongy rippling slightly
segregated no scent I have
scooped through it it
swept through me
spooning out my mind and my
senses melting
slushy mushy part rain
snow sunshine
sleet blending
slowly surely miss my partner
soon to go with her slowly
slipping sliding down a
saliva path now beginning to
    STOP Eating me

—Monique C. Adams, 8th grade

176

SKY

the white stars
fly near the sun
in the sky and
they clutter together
and make signs
maybe they're trying
    to tell us
           something
     I wonder why

     —Charlene Sullivan, 8th grade

(S)(N)
AKES
SN
AKE
SNA
KES
SN
AK
ES
SNA
KESS
NAKE
SSN
AKES
SNA
KES
SNAKE
SSNA
KES
SNA
KES
SNAK
ES
SN
AKE
SSN
AKES
SNAKE
SSNA
KES
SNAKES
I
don't like SNAKES

—Deborah Aylaian, 8th grade

Some people hide in a box
Some people hide in a closet
but Lynn hides behind
her exclamation marks

—Suzanne Avteges, 7th grade

Someone is walking through the snow
Never looking just walking
Over the hills, under the bridges
Wherever the snow will take him.

—Sheila Duffy, 8th grade

SOUNDS OF THE WHALE

I

The subway screeches in
on a foggy rainy night
a man is in the trolley's light
unaware; he hears the cars

then he turns, suddenly,
the conductor jams down his foot
sparks fly out of the soot
He falls in an unearthly scream

II

A moth is fluttering against a window
and someone tosses in his sleep
he wakes up and hears something moving
the moth makes a leap
to avoid a closing window

—Eliot Young, 7th grade

SUPPER

When I was eating supper,
I dropped some food.
My father scolded me and said,
"It's because you were looking the other way."
My younger brother said,
"Yes, it's because you were looking the other way."
A few minutes later
My father dropped some food too.
The whole house became dead silent.

—Ashibe Yoshiaki, age 9

THIS IS MY DREAM

I am a flower. A big
flower. And someone picks
me. I am being split into
pieces and pouring out
blood. But I thought
I am going to die.
And I'll be a seed.

—Sandra B., 5th grade

TREE

I don't want to be a tree.
Somebody saws me.
Something like a needle
comes into my body inch by inch.
Sawdust scatters like blood.
A foot more,
then my body will be cut into two.
Just a little more.
At last I fall down on the ground
as if somebody knocked me down.
Leaves scatter like hair.

—Hamada Tamotsu, age 11

TURKEY

Turkey turkey
listen to me
they're going to
eat you up

—Karen Murphy, 3rd grade

TWELVE WAYS OF LOOKING AT THE NEW YORK STATE THRUWAY FROM SYRACUSE TO BOSTON

1. Syracuse: If I tried
   tearing the road on the
   dotted line,
   the trip might be shorter.

2. Utica: The wheels have been turning
   for only a fragment of time—
   the road winds on—

3. Ithaca: Passing an exit sign,
   I picture a good friend of mine.
   Imagining her as an infant—
   She was born here.
   I laugh about her then
   And the good times now.

4. Schenectady: Repeating the word
   pretending I can spell it
   feels good against my tongue.

5. Albany: I think about New Yorkers,
   their magazines
   and their life.

6. Tollbooth: No longer the
   New York State Thruway—
   Boston's own massive ribbon
   takes over here.

7. Lee: The name is
   incredible contrast to the
   stretch of highway
   left to go.

8. Otis: We welcome you to
   Camp Nowaka
   Mighty glad you're here...

9. Stockbridge: Many summers spent
   on the grass.
   Sounds of Tanglewood music fading—

10. Tollbooth: A man with
    a thin black tie
    and a green suit, takes
    money from my father.
    I wake up.

11. Boston: I can almost taste home
    10 miles away
    and my bed waiting.

12. Driveway: The wheels, and my eyes
    have seen much road.
    We are both tired
    and will rest.

—Lois P. Brody, 9th grade

187

TWINKLE

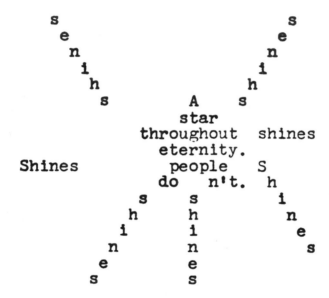

—Bruce Zohn, 8th grade

UH OH

Dear Mom
I know you love ice cream
so when I went to the party
I brought some for you in my
       pocket

—Matt G., 7th grade

UNICORN

Understandable
nice and big
it has a horn on his head
collides with trees
on my trail
runs real fast
noticed me yesterday

—Stephen Lechner, 4th grade

Water falls
At
Their great places
Emptying into little rivers that
Run all over the earth

Frolicking.
Animals run around the falls
Lapping up the water it's
Lip lap lip lap lip lap
Slip slap slip slap slip slop

—Sarah Wolpow, 2nd grade

WAVE WAVEWAVEWAVEWAVEWAVEWAVE WAVEWAVEWAVE WAVEWAVEWAVE WAVEWAVEWAVEWAVE WAVEWAVE WAVEWAVEWAVE WAVEWAVESURFERWAVE WAVEWAVE WAVEWAVE HELP!

—Christopher Dean, 8th grade

we build toward the sky
it does not want us
we want it
clouds pour water on us
snow on us
sleet on us
hail on us
but...
we still build
        up

—Hannibal King, 7th grade

WHAT AM I?

I
am tall
but can be
small. I have limbs,
but cannot walk. I live
for centuries, but can be killed
with powder. I shed, but have no
hair. I cannot think, have no heart, but
I
L
I
V
E

—Doug Robertson, 7th grade

When you're born you don't
know how when or what all
gooey and wet first a little
ship and then you get bigger
and bigger and then your
ship sees a light from the
dark sea. and a big hand reaches
in and grabs you this is the
end it is the real end before you
had been washed overboard but this
was it, you throw the anchor out
and it does not help because they
cut it and then you're hit and you
gulp something in and you start to
begin you gulp and push out
and do it again. but then you're
smothered by blankets. and a few
months after a machine is in front
of you and it flashes a light and
then you start to learn and
learn.

—George Marks, 4th grade

WHERE DID HE GO?

It seems like just yesterday my father was here
Playing games with me after school
But now he can't play games with me anymore
Where did he go? Where did he go?

My father used to help me with my homework
My father used to help me with my chores
My father used to help me with everything
But now he will never again enter my door.
Where did he go? Where did he go?

—Patrick Thebado, 7th grade

WHERE WILL I GO

where will I go
    when I die
in to space
      or
I don't know
I will be lonely though
      come with
        me

      —Kim McCabe, 4th grade

WIND HAS COME WITH THE BIRDS

The chickadee sat in
the tree singing a
song of the long
winter she is just
going to enter. Now
she is coming
back with the
wind of spring
in her wings. It now
of course is spring
with the wind in
your little face,
blowing your golden
hair as you walk
through the fields
with the tall golden
grass, the birds are
coming back of
course, with wind
in their wings as
they flow through
the sky, your little
golden hairs are
swaying in the wind
like little golden
streamers, the wind
of course is 10
breezes in one,
the winds are flying
away for of course
it is summer! Since
summer came too soon
I better leave the wind alone.

—Jillian R., 2nd grade

A WONDER

Everybody watching
Including the deer
So still
Just watching
In the wheat field
Eyes,
Noses,
Ears
All pointed
A wonder

—Margaret Yee, 8th grade

Z is a zerox machine
Y is a yellow zerox machine
X is an x-rated yellow zerox machine
W is a weary x-rated yellow zerox machine
V is a very weary x-rated yellow zerox machine
U is a very weary x-rated yellow zerox machine underneath
T is a t-shaped very weary x-rated yellow zerox machine
   underneath
S is a t-shaped very weary x-rated yellow zerox machine
   underneath that slipped
R is a repeat
Q is a question
P is a popular question
O is an overly popular question
N is a nauseous overly popular question
M is a mini nauseous overly popular question
L is a lamentable mini nauseous overly popular question
K is a kinky lamentable mini nauseous overly popular question
J is junk, what that question became
I is an ingenious place for the junk that the kinky lamentable
   mini nauseous overly popular question became
H is a highly ingenious place for the junk that the kinky
   lamentable mini nauseous overly popular question became
G is a great highly ingenious place for the junk that the kinky
   lamentable mini nauseous overly popular question became
F is where you find it
E is everything you think of
D is the dumby who can't
C is the crusader who does
B is driving you batty
A is the answer (in the zerox machine...)

—Nell Swoish, 8th grade

INDEXES

INDEX OF ADULT POEMS
BY AUTHOR AND TITLE

INDEX OF CHILDREN'S POEMS BY GRADE

9th Grade

Other Children

Hilda Conkling was a gifted child poet of the 1920's. Itozakura Takako, Ashibe Yoshiaki, and Hamada Tomotsu are Japanese children whose poems were anthologized in *There Are Two Lives,* edited by Richard Lewis and translated by Haruna Kimura.

SUBJECT INDEX

ACKNOWLEDGMENTS

Basho: "The Temple Bell Stops," from *The Sea And The Honeycomb: A Book of Tiny Poems,* ed. Robert Bly, copyright © 1971 by Robert Bly. Reprinted by permission of Beacon Press.

Bogan, Louise: "Train Tune," from *The Blue Estuaries,* copyright © 1923, 1929, 1930, 1931, 1933, 1934, 1935, 1936, 1937, 1938, 1941, 1949, 1951, 1952, 1954, 1957, 1958, 1962, 1963, 1964, 1965, 1966, 1967, 1968 by Louise Bogan. Reprinted by permission of Farrar, Straus & Giroux, Inc.

Brooks, Gwendolyn: " 'We Real Cool' The Pool Players. Seven at the Golden Shovel.," from *The World of Gwendolyn Brooks* (1971), copyright © 1959 by Gwendolyn Brooks. Reprinted by permission of Harper & Row, Publishers, Inc.

Bruchac, Joseph: "First Deer," from *New Campus Writing* (Miller), McGraw-Hill Book Company. Reprinted by permission of McGraw-Hill Book Company.

Cloutier, David: "Shaman's Incantation To Exorcise A Demon," from *Spirit, Spirit: Shaman Songs, Incantations* (Copper Beech, 1973), version from the Yukaghir by David Cloutier. Reprinted by permission of David Cloutier.

Conkling, Hilda: "The Cellar," from *Shoes Of The Wind* (Stokes, Lippincott, 1922), copyright © 1949 by Hilda Conkling. Reprinted by permission of Hilda Conkling.

Cornish, Sam: "Sam's World," from *Natural Process,* ed. Ted Willentz and Tom Weatherly, copyright © 1970 by Hill and Wang, Inc. Reprinted with the permission of Hill and Wang (now a division of Farrar, Straus & Giroux, Inc.)

Döhl, Reinhard: "Apfel," from *An Anthology of Concrete Poetry,* ed. Emmett Williams, (Something Else Press, Inc., 1967). Reprinted by permission of Reinhard Döhl.

Draper, George: "Rink Keeper's Sestina: Hockey, hockey," copyright © 1975 by The Atlantic Monthly Company, Boston, Mass. Reprinted with permission.

Eliot, T.S.: "Cape Ann," from *Collected Poems 1909-1962,* by T.S. Eliot, copyright © 1936 by Harcourt Brace Jovanovich, Inc.; copyright 1963, 1964 by T.S. Eliot. Reprinted by permission of the publishers.

Ferlinghetti, Lawrence: "Fortune has its cookies to give out," from *A Coney Island Of The Mind,* copyright © 1955 by Lawrence Ferlinghetti. Reprinted by permission of New Directions Publishing Corporation.

Fox, Siv Cedering: "Hands," from *Cup Of Cold Water.* (New Rivers Press), copyright © 1973 by Siv Cedering Fox. Reprinted by permission of Siv Cedering Fox.

Francis, Robert: "Blue Cornucopia," from *Like Ghosts of Eagles* (University of Massachusetts Press, 1974), copyright © 1974 by Robert Francis. Reprinted by permission of the author and the University of Massachusetts Press; "Hallelujah: A Sestina," from *The Orb Weaver,* copyright © 1960 by Robert Francis. Reprinted by permission of Wesleyan University Press.

Gensler, Kinereth: "Clock," copyright © 1974 by Kinereth Gensler. This poem appeared originally in *The Andover Review.* Reprinted by permission of Kinereth Gensler.

Giovanni, Nikki: "Knoxville, Tennessee," from *Black Feeling, Black Talk, Black Judgement,* copyright © 1968, 1970 by Nikki Giovanni. Reprinted by permission of William Morrow & Co., Inc.

Hall, Donald: "Self-Portrait, As A Bear," from *The Alligator Bride* (Harper & Row Publishers, 1969), copyright © 1969 by Donald Hall. Reprinted by permission of Donald Hall.

9 8 7 5